COMPACT
CYMRU

The Great Trains of Wales
explored

Arfon Haines Davies

Gwasg Carreg Gwalch

First published in 2017
© text: Arfon Haines Davies
© Images: Crown copyright (2016) Visit Wales;
Pierino Algieri; Keith O'Brien
© publication: Gwasg Carreg Gwalch 2017

ISBN: 978-1-84524-260-2
Cover design: Eleri Owen
Map: Alison Davies
Published by Gwasg Carreg Gwalch,
12 Iard yr Orsaf, Llanrwst, Wales LL26 0EH
tel: 01492 642031
email: llanrwst@carreg-gwalch.com
website: www.carreg-gwalch.com

Dedication

This book is dedicated with thanks and huge respect to the army of volunteers whose hard work, commitment and enthusiasm make it possible for us all to enjoy our wonderful heritage railways ... Diolch.

Acknowledgements

The author is grateful to Visit Wales for their photographs; to Pierino Algieri for photographs on pages 1, 10, 11, 48, 49, 55, 56, 59, 72, 74, 76, 78, 80; Keith O'Brien for photographs on pages 8, 16, 26, 27, 36, 37, 86, 87; Ray Wood pages 44, 48; Penrhyn Rail Ltd page 52; John R. Jones pages 82-88; Vale of Rheidol Archive Collection 88; Kevin Heywood page 91.

Talyllyn Railway

Contents

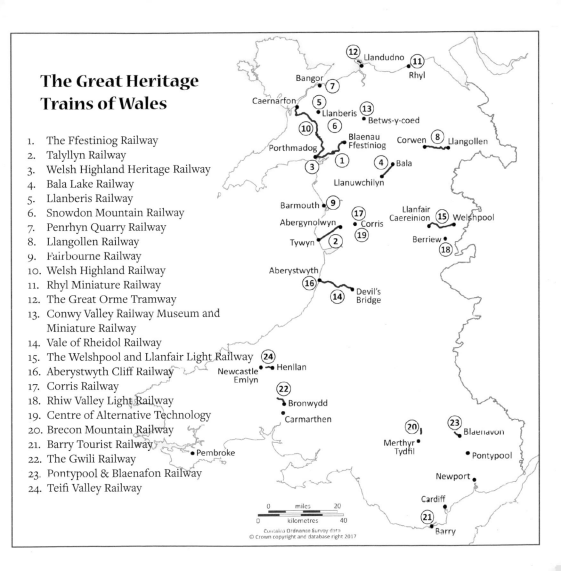

Introduction

I am often asked where and when did my interest in railways and in particular steam engines begin. The answers are quite simple Aberystwyth and 1953. My father was a Wesleyan Methodist minister and as was the pattern in those days he would be relocated every five years to a different circuit and chapel. And so it was in September 1953 when my father became minister at St Pauls, Aberystwyth. I had just turned five years old and one of my first memories of Aberystwyth is being taken by my father for a trip on the Vale of Rheidol railway. The rest as they say is history.

I was very fortunate to be a pupil at Aberystwyth Welsh junior school in Alexandra Road which was conveniently located parallel to Aberystwyth station. The highlight of the day for me, I'm somewhat ashamed to admit, was when the bell would ring at about 3.30 and a gang of us would climb over the station wall to await the arrival of the Cambrian Coast Express. I do not recall that we ever had to wait too long as it always seemed to be on time, hauled by an immaculate Manor Class locomotive. The staff at Aberystwyth shed took great pride in the appearance of their locos especially the one allocated to haul the Cambrian Coast Express. The buffer would be brilliant white as would the handles on the smokebox and the brass work polished to perfection. This was especially true of the nameplates, and as a child I remember thinking did places like Compton Manor and Broome Manor really exist because, if they did, they were certainly not in the Aberystwyth area!

During my childhood I never missed an opportunity to stop and visit one of the Welsh narrow gauge railways if we were travelling around Wales in my dad's old Austin 10. I'm surprised that my father did not try to work out an alternative route to avoid all railways! Having said that I was easily pleased and always quite content just to spend a few minutes admiring the steam loco, there was always a sense of magic about the occasion.

In the mid 70s I was once again

1. *Arfon Haines Davies when he was honoured as President of Gwili Railway;* 2. *On the footplate of Prince, Ffestiniog Railway, mid-1950s ...* 3. *... and a further footplate experience on the Flying Scotsman at Llangollen in 1993*

extremely fortunate to get what was for me the dream job of working as a presenter with HTV Wales, which I did for well over 30 years ... much to the surprise of many! One of the 'perks' was being allowed to film items and indeed series about railways in Wales. This would allow me to have 'access to all areas' and I was often allowed to travel on the footplate ... talk about a labour of love!

Even though sixty years have passed since those halcyon days on Aber station, I can honestly say that I still get the same sense of excitement and awe when I visit one of our wonderful heritage railways. We are so fortunate in Wales to have so many that provide the ideal opportunity to enjoy some of the most spectacular scenery in the world. From the mountains of Snowdonia to the Brecon National Park and from the vale of Clwyd to the vale of Rheidol, these heritage railways are, in my mind without doubt, the jewel in the Welsh crown.

1. The Ffestiniog Railway

Ffestiniog Railway is the oldest surviving railway company in the world, being founded by an act of parliament in 1832. Four years later it opened to carry slate from the quarries of Blaenau Ffestiniog to the harbour at Porthmadog, where it was loaded onto ships and transported all over the world. The railway was graded so that the loaded wagons could be run by gravity downhill all the way to Porthmadog, and then the empty wagons were pulled back up by horses.

In 1860 the board of the company began to investigate the possibility of introducing steam locomotives. Numerous tests were carried out and in 1863 after the track had been modernised, steam locomotives were introduced. This lead to the official carrying of passengers.

Unfortunately by the 1920s the demand for slate as roofing material dropped due to the advent of newer materials, as a result the railway suffered a gradual decline in traffic. The only encouraging aspect was that the numbers of passengers carried was considerably increased by tourists who came from far and wide to enjoy the spectacular scenery visible from the train as it passed through the vale of Ffestiniog. Sadly the passenger service was withdrawn with the outbreak of the Second World War in 1939. Slate trains continued to run as required and when motive power was available throughout the war years. On 1 August 1946 slate traffic ceased apart from a short section which was leased to the quarry owners in Blaenau Ffestiniog.

In 1949, various groups of enthusiasts attempted to reopen the railway. It was a long hard fought struggle, but on 23 July 1955 the first public passenger service from Porthmadog along the cob to Boston Lodge was re-opened. During the following years, thanks in no small part to a band of hard working volunteers, the railway slowly worked its way back to Blaenau Ffestiniog. There were numerous obstacles along the way, including the ambitious Llyn Ystradau deviation, which

Overleaf: Oakeley Quarry, Blaenau Ffestiniog – one of the sources of Ffestiniog Railway slate

was constructed between 1965 and 1978 in order to avoid the works at Ffestiniog Power Station. The dream of returning to Blaenau Ffestiniog became a reality in 1982, a wonderful way of celebrating the 150th anniversary of the royal assent to Ffestiniog Railway in 1832.

My first memory of the Ffestiniog railway would have been during the late 50s, travelling as a family from Aberystwyth to visit my grandparents in Caernarfon. I would have been 7 or 8 years old at the time, and I can even remember my father's car, an old Austin 10 which we affectionately called *Jalope* – still don't

know why. During the painstakingly long journey sitting in the cramped back seat of the car I would have been wishing and hoping that when we reached the approach to Porthmadog, known as the cob, that there would be a train travelling on the tracks which ran parallel to the main road. I would then encourage my dad to race the train. Such recklessness – and my father a Wesleyan Minister!

The Ffestiniog railway is located mainly within Snowdonia National Park, and the 13½ mile journey takes us from the

Overleaf: Porthmadog Cob; Llyn Ystradau; Tan-y-bwlch and Tanygrisiau stations

harbour of Porthmadog to the slate town of Blaenau Ffestiniog. It is a journey that takes the passenger from the coast to the mountains, through some of the most spectacular scenery you could imagine. Pastures give way to trees as you steam through the vale of Ffestiniog passing ancient woodlands, streams and waterfalls, before reaching the rows of quaint cottages and dramatic slate tips at Blaenau Ffestiniog – 'The town that roofed the world'.

The journey takes around an hour and a quarter, as it climbs over 700 feet (213 metres) to its destination. Along the way

there is plenty of opportunity to leave the train and do some exploring and then continue the journey on a later train. There are stations as Minffordd and Tanygrisiau as well as numerous request stops.

As a youngster one of the things that made the Ffestiniog special for me were the Double Fairlie locomotives, which still seem to be as popular as ever with visitors. The steam engine equivalent of Dr Doolittle's push-me-pull-you. But instead of having a head on either end this one has a chimney!

As well as regular services there are

special events arranged throughout the year. It's well worth checking the excellent website *www.festrail.co.uk*

End of the line at Blaenau Ffestiniog

2. Talyllyn Railway

The Talyllyn Railway was opened in 1866. Including branches, it was about 10 miles (16.09 km) long and was designed to carry slate from the Bryn Eglwys Quarries to a wharf alongside the Cambrian Coast Line at Tywyn. It was originally proposed that the railway should terminate at Aberdovey to take advantage of the harbour there, but the construction of the Cambrian Coast Line meant that the plans had to be modified.

The engineer was James Swinton Spooner, son of James Spooner who had built the Ffestiniog Railway. The Act of Parliament in 1865 which granted permission to build the railway also authorised passenger services, the first time that this had been authorised on a narrow gauge line.

Talyllyn railway was unusual compared to other narrow gauge railways built to serve the slate industry, in the fact that it was owned by the only quarry it served and also ran a public passenger service. On opening the minimum of equipment was provided, two locomotives *Talyllyn* and *Dolgoch*, and just four carriages, a van and some wagons.

By 1879 it was obvious that the venture was not a success, and attempts were made to sell both quarry and railway at auction, but this proved unsuccessful. The quarry and railway were finally bought by William McConnel. For a few years the railway and quarry flourished but with leases on the land running out it was decided in 1909 to close it. The railway and quarry were then taken over by the local MP, Sir Henry Hadden Jones, and he managed to keep the railway going until his death in 1950. There had been little or no investment in the line for a number of years, and visitors could expect a 1 in 10 chance of derailment on their journey, as it appeared that the only thing that held the track in place was the grass! It seemed to everyone that the only future for the Talyllyn would be closure.

In 1950 there were no preserved railways, even attempts to reopen the Ffestiniog railway using volunteers had failed. Fortunately for the Talyllyn a group of enthusiasts under the leadership of the engineer and author Tom Rolt held a public meeting in Birmingham and the

Talyllyn Railway Preservation Society was born. Sir Henry's widow, Lady Hadden, agreed to hand over the railway to the society whilst maintaining ownership of the Quarry.

On 14 May 1951 the Talyllyn Railway Preservation Society ran its first public service, a historical day for railway preservation. Since then the railway has gone from strength to strength culminating in the opening of an extension towards the old quarry in Nant Gwernol in 1976.

To many of us the story of the Talyllyn railway could be described as a fairy-tale. From its humble beginnings when a group of enthusiasts got together in Birmingham under the guidance of Tom Rolt, to the successful tourist attraction it has become today. As the world's first preserved railway I can only imagine with envy what it must have been like for those stalwart pioneering volunteers back in the early 1950s. Here I have to make a confession and say that if I was asked to chose a favourite railway book, one of them most certainly would be L.T.C. Rolt's *Railway Adventure* which has become a classic of railway literature. If you can get hold of a

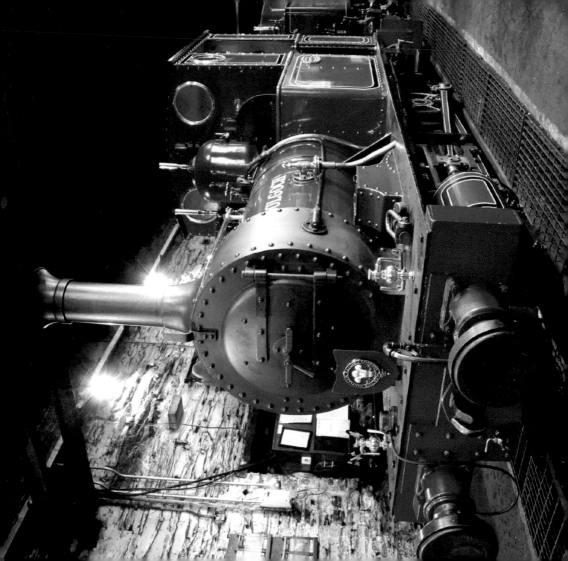

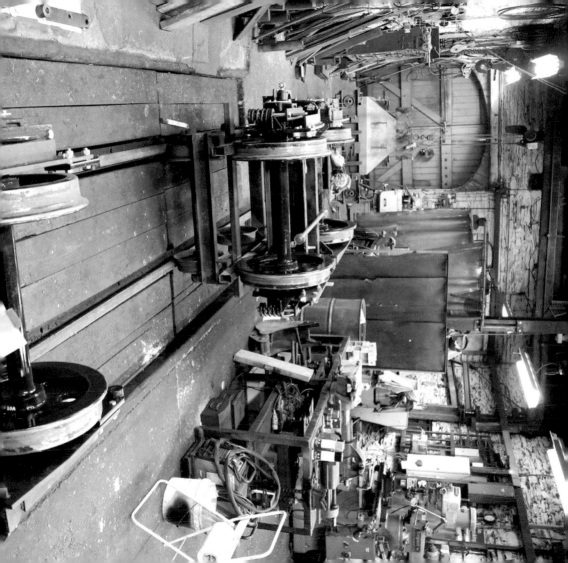

copy I promise you will not be disappointed! To continue with the fairy-tale theme, renowned railway artist Terence Cuneo's idyllic painting of Dolgoch station must come high on the list of most popular railway posters ... you can almost smell the steam!

The Talyllyn journey starts at Tywyn wharf, conveniently situated next to the main line station. Along the route, stations of interest include Rhydyronen, a charming little station in delightful surroundings. As well as serving the local village the station is a good starting place for mountain walks.

One of the most popular stop-off points is Dolgoch which gives passengers the opportunity to visit the magnificent falls. The journey then continues to Abergynolwyn, the main inland station where facilities include a Tea Room, shop and toilets, before terminating at Nant Gwernol. This station is situated in a natural ravine, and has no road access, it can only be reached by means of the forest walk or the footpath from the car park in Abergynolwyn both of which are unsuitable for the elderly or disabled.

The last time I visited the railway was a few years ago to film an item for *Heno*, a

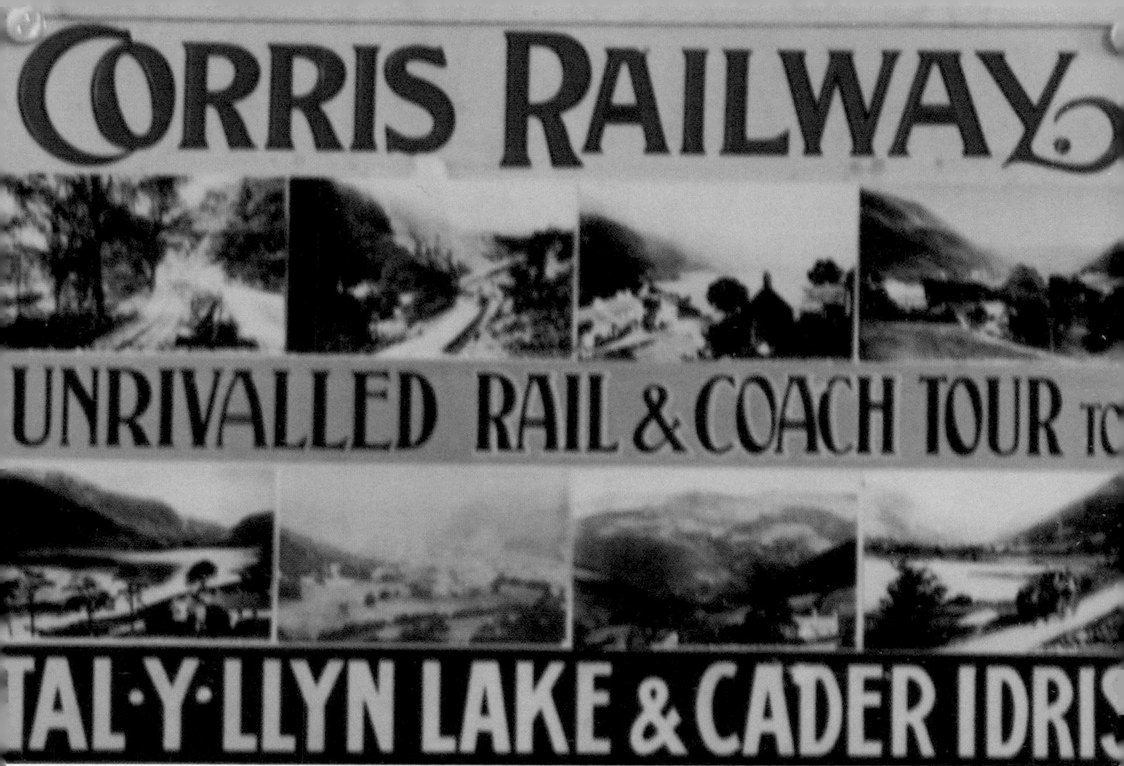

CORRIS RAILWAYS

UNRIVALLED RAIL & COACH TOUR TO

TAL·Y·LLYN LAKE & CADER IDRIS

popular magazine programme on S4C, and I have to say I spent a most enjoyable hour or so in the museum which I would most definitely recommend. As well as locomotives, signalling equipment, paperwork and tickets there is also a special section devoted to the Reverend W. V. Awdry, creator of Thomas the Tank Engine. Awdry was an early volunteer at the Talyllyn railway and even worked as a guard. The history of the railway and his experiences in those early days were the inspiration for his Skarloey Railway in the Thomas the Tank Engine stories. In the museum there is a reconstruction of the Reverend Awdry's study from his last home in Stroud, Gloucestershire, complete with typewriter and hundreds of his books. As we were filming I had the honour and privilege of being allowed to sit behind the desk, an experience which I found truly emotional. To think that those stories about Thomas and his friends which had delighted me as a child had been written on that very typewriter!

To me the spirit of people like the Reverend Awdry, Tom Rolt and Sir Henry epitomise everything that is so wonderful about the Talyllyn railway. It may well be the first preserved railway in the world but it has most definitely not rested on its laurels.

3. Welsh Highland Heritage Railway

The Welsh Highland Heritage Railway (WHHR) (not to be mistaken with the Welsh Highland Railway, see page 64) is situated opposite the mainline station at Porthmadog. Work on the line started in the 1970s and it runs alongside the Cambrian Coast Line at a location known as Beddgelert sidings.

The journey is a mile (1.6 km in length) as far as Pen y Mount, where there is a small 1920s style replica station. On the return journey the train stops at Gelert's Farm Halt, allowing passengers to visit the Heritage Centre and take a ride on the 7¼ inch gauge miniature railway.

There is also an opportunity to find out more about the area's slate industry and railways. The WHHR prides itself on being able to offer an experience which is not only fun, but also as 'hands on' as it can be. It is ideally suited for families with young children who may get bored on a long journey.

No visit is complete without a call at the station gift shop which stocks an amazing range of railway books, toys and souvenirs.

The fully licensed Tea Room is also worth a visit, where you can feast on a Fireman's Breakfast, a Porter's Lunch or a traditional Welsh Cream Tea.

For a comparatively small railway, it certainly does seem to pack an awful lot into it. Run almost entirely by volunteers in their spare time one certainly gets the impression that they want the visitor to have as much fun and enjoyment as they do. An ethic to be applauded.

The Great Trains of Wales

4. Bala Lake Railway

Rheilffordd Llyn Tegid (Bala Lake Railway) is a 9 mile (14½ km) return journey alongside Llyn Tegid (Bala lake), through Snowdonia National Park and offering some of the most impressive and beautiful scenery that Wales has to offer.

The railway runs on the former secondary through route from Ruabon to Barmouth, with the line between Ruabon and Dolgellau being operated by the Great Western Railway, and from Dolgellau to Barmouth by the Cambrian Railways, the whole becoming Great Western in the amalgamation in 1922. The branch line which was closed in 1965 with the track being lifted three years later.

By 1971 plans were afoot to build a narrow gauge railway on the lakeside trackbed, and a company, Rheilffordd Llyn Tegid Cyf. (the first to be registered in Welsh), was formed.

A year later the first train ran as far as Pentrepiod, 1½ miles (2.5 km) from Llanuwchllyn. By 1976 the railway had reached Penybont, the site of Bala Lake Halt.

The journey takes approximately an hour starting from the railway's headquarters at Llanuwchllyn which features an original Great Western signal box, that is often open to visitors. In the village of Llanuwchllyn is a prominent statue of the founder of Urdd Gobaith Cymru (the Welsh youth movement), Sir Ifan ab Owen Edwards, standing with his

father O. M. Edwards, both born in the village.

After leaving the village the line descends down to Pentrepiod, a request halt offers the traveller the opportunity to alight and access the lakeside for walks, picnics and bird watching. From here the line climbs steadily before dropping down through a wooded cutting to join the lakeside again. The journey really does offer extensive panoramic views of the lake as well as the imposing Aran mountain range, not to mention the chance of sighting buzzards and herons.

The end of the line is Bala (Penybont), where trains usually wait for 10 minutes whilst the engine is run around and passengers have the opportunity of visiting Bala town for shopping or maybe a Welsh tea in one of the cafes. Llyn Tegid is the largest natural body of water in Wales. It is 4 miles (6.4 km) long, by a mile (1.6 km) wide. Many a happy hour I spent as a child enjoying boat trips, while staying at the Urdd residential camp at Glanllyn on the other side of the lake. The lake is also home for the rare 'Gwyniad' fish, the species that became trapped in the lake at the end of the last Ice Age, and is only found in Llyn Tegid.

There is no doubt that the railway provides the ideal centrepiece for a visit to Llyn Tegid, and as they proudly proclaim in their brochure it really is 'a perfect day out'.

The Bala Lake Railway now has the largest single collection of ex-quarry *Hunslet* locomotives anywhere in the world. These were particularly synonymous with the Penrhyn Quarry in Bethesda and the Dinorwig Quarry in Llanberis, the largest and second largest slate quarries in the world respectively. Four of the engines worked at Dinorwig, including *Holy War* which was the last steam engine to work in a slate quarry anywhere in Britain, being withdrawn from service in November 1967. The fifth engine *Winifred* worked at the Penrhyn Quarry, and after withdrawal was sold and exported to the USA where she spent almost fifty years in storage, completely untouched. She returned to Wales in 2012 still wearing the same worn coat of paint that she had when she left and on examining her ashpan, the remains of the last fire was also found. She and *Holy War*, are among the six currently operational steam engines at Llanuwchllyn.

5. Llanberis Lake Railway

The railway runs along part of the old Padarn Railway which connected the Dinorwig Quarry with the harbour at Y Felinheli.

Following the closure of the railway in 1961 various plans were made to open a narrow gauge tourist railway on the track-bed. It was proposed to run a railway that would circle Llyn Padarn and also use the track-bed of the British Rail Llanberis branch line, but this did not come to fruition.

A shorter railway, running from the quarry company workshops at Gilfach Ddu along the eastern side of the lake to Penllyn was proposed in 1966. Three years later the quarry closed and the railway company purchased three steam locomotives and one diesel for use on the planned railway. It was officially opened in 1971 and by the end of the first season more than thirty thousand passengers had been carried.

In 2003 the railway was extended to Llanberis with a new station close to the Snowdon Mountain Railway.

Llyn Padarn is also home to a variety of fish including a rare arctic char called the *torgoch*. Clearly visible at the start of the journey is Dolbadarn castle built early in the 13th century by Llywelyn Fawr. From here the train runs non-stop through Padarn Country Park (*Parc Gwledig Padarn*), joining the 1845 slate railway route along the shores of Llyn Padarn as far as Penllyn.

The 5 mile (8 km) return trip takes around an hour and there is also an opportunity to stop on the way at Cei

Llydan for a lakeside picnic and catch a later train back.

No visit to Llanberis would be complete without calling in at the National Slate Museum, sited in the Victorian workshop built in the shadow of Elidir mountain. During your visit you will have the opportunity of seeing demonstrations including the art of slate splitting. If you are invited to 'have a go' all I can say is that it's most definitely not as easy as it looks ... you have been warned!

6. Snowdon Mountain Railway

Since its opening in 1896 visitors have been travelling to Llanberis in the heart of Snowdonia National Park to travel on the world famous Snowdon Mountain Railway. The mountain is the highest peak in Wales and England and the railway was built solely for the purpose of tourism. Despite a disastrous start to its history which resulted in a derailment, the railway seems to have gone from strength to strength and certainly warrants the old adage of 'book early to avoid disappointment'.

As you journey up to the summit the scenery can only be described as truly breathless. The weather certainly makes a huge difference and there does not seem to be a fool proof way of forecasting as far as Snowdon is concerned. I have often felt that a toss of a coin could be more accurate. Many a time I've left Llanberis on a journey to the summit with a back drop of Mediterranean conditions only to be met half way up by a wall of dark menacing clouds and limited visibility –

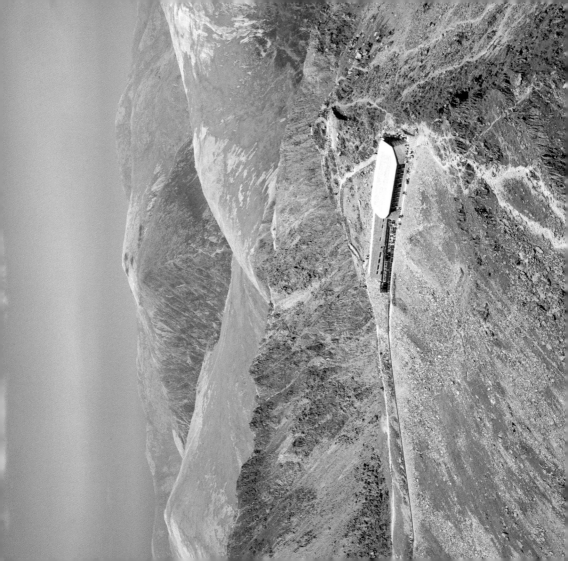

surprisingly it can also happen the other way around.

In 1998 an appeal was set up to buy more than 4,000 acres of the southern flank of Snowdon. Days before the deadline the National Trust announced that the amount pledged in donation had reached the £4 million target. The President of the appeal, Anthony Hopkins, himself, donated £1 million, saying that Snowdonia is one of the most beautiful places in the world and Snowdon is the jewel that lies at its heart'.

The carriages for the railway were built in England, but the three steam

locomotives were ordered from Switzerland, the centre of mountain railway expertise. The track used is also of Swiss design and is the only system of its kind in the UK. Using rack-and-pinion, which means each locomotive is equipped with toothed cog wheels which engage the rack, provide all the traction necessary to climb the steep incline to the summit.

Today the tourist has the choice of travelling on the loose traditional diesel service or the Heritage Steam experience, which uses one of the original steam locomotives from 1896. Whichever service you use it's well worth booking in advance,

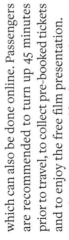

which can also be done online. Passengers are recommended to turn up 45 minutes prior to travel, to collect pre-booked tickets and to enjoy the free film presentation.

The journey itself takes an hour to reach Hafod Eryri, the Snowdon Summit Visitor Centre, with half an hour allowed at the summit before starting on the return journey to Llanberis. In April 2006 Snowdonia National Park Authority with the support of Snowdon Mountain Railway and other share-holders agreed a deal to start work on a new cafe and visitor centre. Hafod Eryri was officially opened on 12 June 2009.

Much has been written of the views from the summit, on a clear day it's possible to see Blackpool tower and even as far as the Lake District. What makes the summit special for me is to just sit and take a few minutes to try and take it all in, the feeling that you are sitting on top of the world (well Wales anyway!). Many have said it is quite an emotional experience – this I can understand. It is certainly a magical experience, one that has been savoured by some 12 million intrepid explorers since 1896.

7. Penrhyn Quarry Railway

The Penrhyn Quarry Railway first opened as the Llandegai Tramway in 1798 becoming the Penrhyn Railway in 1801. It was built to carry slate from the quarries at Bethesda to Port Penrhyn at Bangor. The line is the oldest narrow gauge railway in Wales, but sadly closed in 1962.

Fifty years later restoration of a section of the original railway at Felin Fawr was completed. The section of restored railway is approximately one fifth of a mile in length and runs between Coed-y-Park Bridge (*Felin Fawr*) and Saint Anns. 'Open Weekends' with public running have been held annually from 2013 and during the summer months of 2016 a regular Diesel Hauled Weekend Service was being run.

8. Llangollen Railway

The Llangollen Railway is the longest preserved standard gauge railway in Wales. The ten mile journey from Llangollen to Corwen takes approximately three quarters of an hour.

Located within an Area of Outstanding Natural Beauty the line follows the river Dee and meanders along the magnificent Dee valley. The history of the line begins in the mid 19th century when a number of schemes were proposed to connect Llangollen to the rail network.

The route from Ruabon to Barmouth was a secondary route across Wales. The preferred scheme was the vale of Llangollen Railway, engineered by Henry Robertson whose bill received Royal Assent in 1859. The line branched off the main Shrewsbury to Chester line just south of Ruabon and opened to passengers three years later in 1862. The development of the line west of Llangollen was by the Llangollen and Corwen Railway.

Even as the line was opened plans were already underway to extend the line from Llangollen to the small market town of Corwen, some ten miles away. On 8 May 1865, the line from Llangollen to Corwen was officially opened.

The line's history up to closure is similar to that of numerous other lines; opening in the mid 19th century, expanding and enjoying commercial success and then suffering a decline from the late 1930s onwards. In the 1960s the Beeching axe fell on far too many lines in Wales and this was the case with the Llangollen to Corwen section, final services finishing on 1 April 1968.

The revival began in 1972 just four years after the closure of the line, when a group of enthusiasts calling themselves 'The Flint and Deeside Railway Preservation Society' had the idea of running a preserved standard gauge railway in northern Wales.

On 1 July 1975, the society gained access to the site and work began in earnest to reopen the line the following September.

Numerous times whilst writing about preserved railways I mention the hard

work and dedication of volunteers – never has this been truer than with the Llangollen railway. As all the track had been lifted almost immediately after closure, new track had to be found, locomotives and rolling stock had to be acquired. There must have been times when those stalwart volunteers thought that reopening the line as far as Corwen was a fanciful dream! Their determination must have been incredible because by October 1985 the first passenger train to run to Berwyn in twenty years set off from Llangollen.

Work on rebuilding the line continued; firstly, to Deeside halt, then Glyndyfrdwy, Carrog and the final run to Corwen Central terminus in 2018. Irrespective of the time of year you decide to visit the line there really is an incredible amount to do. From a 'Day out with Thomas' or a 'Teddy Bears Picnic' to the 'Steam and Jazz Train', 'Real Ale Train' or the highly popular 'Santa Specials'. It really is worth checking on the excellent website.

Over the years I have been very fortunate to have filmed on the line a number of times. On one memorable occasion I had to act as fireman on the

footplate of one of my favourite locomotives, 7822 *Foxcote Manor*. It was probably one of the hardest jobs I have ever had to do, but I actually thought I had coped rather well. At the end of filming I remember asking the driver whether he thought my firing skills were good enough to get the engine up the notorious Talerddig climb on the Aberystwyth to Shrewsbury Cambrian Coast express route. His answer was short, 'Talerddig? You wouldn't have got it out of Aberystwyth Station!' (or words to that effect!).

Having disgraced myself in such a manner it came as a great surprise to me a few years later on 4 July 2006 when I was invited back to officially open the newly refurbished Llangollen station. It was a great honour and I can only surmise that for whatever reason I was asked back it was certainly nothing to do with my firing skills!

One of the most popular activities offered by the railway is the 'driver experience'. I have often been asked, what was the best Christmas present I have ever received? Certainly high on that list would be one which I received from my parents in 1995, it was a 'drivers experience' on the Llangollen Railway with visiting locomotive, *Flying Scotsman*, and what an experience it was! Unforgettable!

One of the things that the Llangollen is proud of is that it's 'more than a railway', and how true that is. You can now get married in the Henry Robertson Suite on Llangollen station, and then after the service, enjoy your wedding breakfast onboard your own private carriage where you can sit back and enjoy the splendid scenery. You can even stay in the beautifully renovated, grade two listed, station master's house, which is situated right on the platform on Berwyn station.

A trip on the Llangollen railway certainly takes you back to a more relaxed and uncomplicated era. The beautifully restored idyllic stations on the route give the traveller the opportunity to stop a while and enjoy a cuppa and cake at one of the tea rooms. One thing I can say from experience is that you will most definitely receive the warmest of welcomes.

Carrog bridge and Glyndyfrdwy

9. Fairbourne Railway

Fairbourne Railway is one of Wales' smallest heritage railways, but despite its size it has an interesting and varied history. It actually started life as a 2 foot gauge horse tramway in the 1890s. The reason for its existence was to help with the development of Fairbourne as a holiday resort, and compete with the highly popular Barmouth on the other side of the estuary.

In 1916 the line was converted to a 15 inch gauge steam railway. It had mixed fortunes during the inter-war years and at one time it was leased by the ferry men. Sadly, in 1940, after operating a diesel service for its final year, it closed.

Following the war the railway was in a severely damaged state but in 1946 it was rescued by a consortium of Midlands businessmen lead by John Wilkins, owner of the Servis Washing Machine Company. Miraculously the following year the line reopened and thanks to his generosity new steam and diesel locomotives were acquired.

My personal memories of the line go back to the 1960s which would have been the heyday of the railway. A journey on the Fairbourne was a real adventure for a young school boy, combining a journey on both land and sea!

I remember I would always try and manage to obtain the nearest seat to the engine and in my imagination pretend that I was the driver's assistant! On arrival at the end of the line at Barmouth Ferry Station we would as a family nervously look out over the estuary to try and ascertain whether it was going to be a rough or a smooth crossing. Unfortunately all the memories I have are of stormy seas and a fairly small boat as well. One aspect of the journey I do remember well is the relief of stepping out on *terra firma* once the journey had been completed.

During the 1970s and 80s there was a steady decline in passenger numbers on the Fairbourne Railway and in 1984 the line's ownership changed once more. This time not only was there a change in ownership but also in the railway's gauge, and in 1986 four new steam locomotives were introduced on the now 12¼ inch railway.

The Fairbourne Railway was again put up for sale in 1990 with the line's fortunes declining once again. Five years later, and with the line now having deteriorated dramatically, the line was eventually bought by the late Prof. Tony and Mrs Atkinson and Dr and Mrs Melton.

From 2009 the ownership of the railway was transferred to a charitable body in order to preserve its long term future.

On my visits to Fairbourne one thing that becomes very noticeable is just how popular this line is with children. One cannot fail to be enthralled by all the excitement and joy they experience on a journey. Add to that the wonderful panoramic views of Cardigan Bay and Snowdonia, not forgetting the majestic Barmouth Bridge which crosses the Mawddach estuary. Never has the old adage 'great things come in small packages' been truer than in conjunction with the Fairbourne Railway.

Enjoy your journey and if you are thinking of taking the ferry over the Mawddach to Barmouth – let's hope for a smooth crossing!

10. Welsh Highland Railway

The history of the Welsh Highland Railway dates back to 1922 with the merger of the North Wales Narrow Gauge Railways and the Portmadoc, Beddgelert, and South Snowdon Railway. Sadly the Welsh Highland Railway was not a successful railway, there were problems right from the very beginning. It had hoped to capitalise on the traffic from the flourishing slate quarries, but sadly it was not long before they were in decline. Its passenger services also proved to be unsuccessful with local bus services providing a quicker and more efficient service. Its rolling stock was also out of date and in 1924 winter passenger services were discontinued due to poor traffic. There was also a dispute with the Great Western Railway over the costs of the crossing over its line in Porthmadog. One thing lead to another and in 1927 the county council sued and put the railway into receivership. The railway continued to provide a service, but by 1933 it was so run down that the local authorities decided to close it. In 1934 the company

agreed to lease the line to the Ffestiniog Railway Company, but this proved to be a disaster with the Ffestiniog Railway having to pay rent even if the Welsh Highland Railway made a loss.

The Ffestiniog Railway did their best to revive the flagging popularity of the line by concentrating on the tourist market. These attempts also proved to be unsuccessful with the last passenger service running in 1936 and the last goods service in 1937. The Welsh Highland Railway was bankrupt and the line became dormant with most of the rolling stock being sold off. By 1941 most of the track between Dinas and Croesor junction was lifted, but the remainder was left in case the Croesor quarries reopened after the war. This was not to be and by 1950 the track had been lifted.

The restoration of the Welsh Highland Railway has without doubt been a long and complicated journey. Attempts to reinstate the railway were first made in the 1960s and since then there have been numerous court cases and public enquires.

At first the Ffestiniog Railway Company were concerned about the possible competition from a rebuilt Welsh Highland Railway and in 1987 a confidential bid was made by the Ffestiniog Railway Company to buy the Welsh Highland Railway track-bed from the official receiver to prevent any development of the Welsh Highland Railway. However in 1990 the Ffestiniog Railway Company had a change of heart and decided to take over the restoration of the railway. In 1997 the section to Dinas was opened; this was followed by the opening of sections to Waunfawr, Rhyd-ddu, Beddgelert, Hafod y Llyn, Pont Croesor and then finally in 2011 the line was completed when it reached Porthmadog Harbour.

As I was born in Caernarfon (hence the name Arfon) it will come as no surprise that this line is also one that means a great deal to me. One of my favourite railway sections has always been the standard gauge line from Caernarfon to Afonwen, sadly closed during the Beeching era. It was immortalised in a song by famous Welsh singer Bryn Fôn, when he cleverly mentions some of the stations and halts on the route such as Bryncir, Chwilog and Penygroes. The first section of the Welsh Highland Railway to Dinas follows the original London and North Western Railway standard gauge route and there can be no more impressive a sight in the preservation era than seeing one of the enormous Welsh Highland Railway *Garratt* locomotives climbing out of Caernarfon with the magnificent castle as a backdrop (even more impressive for the passenger on the return journey, especially if you are sitting on the left hand side). The distinguished Welsh artist, William Selwyn, has perfectly captured this scene numerous times in his wonderful atmospheric watercolour paintings. The Welsh Highland Railway is the longest heritage railway in the UK covering some 25 miles (40 km) and taking 2¼ hours in duration. It travels through some of the most impressive scenery in the world before reaching its destination at the harbour town of Porthmadog.

For the visitor who wants to take a shorter journey it's possible to stop at many of the halts and stations along the way. A popular destination is the village of

Beddgelert which is 1½ hours from Caernarfon and 45 minutes from Porthmadog. The village has some wonderful and traditional pubs and shops and offers the opportunity to take a leisurely river walk. Without doubt the most popular attraction in the village is Gelert's grave. Legend has it that Prince Llywelyn killed his faithful dog Gelert with his sword when he thought the dog had attacked and killed his son, sadly he was to realise later that the dog had in fact saved his son from a vicious wolf. The grave lies in the meadows near the river Glaslyn. I also have to note that as the 1959 film *Inn of the Sixth Happiness*, staring Ingrid Bergman is my favourite film, that this was actually filmed in the surrounding area, with Snowdonia substituting for the mountain ranges of China. If you decide to take the full journey to Porthmadog you will find it's a town steeped in maritime

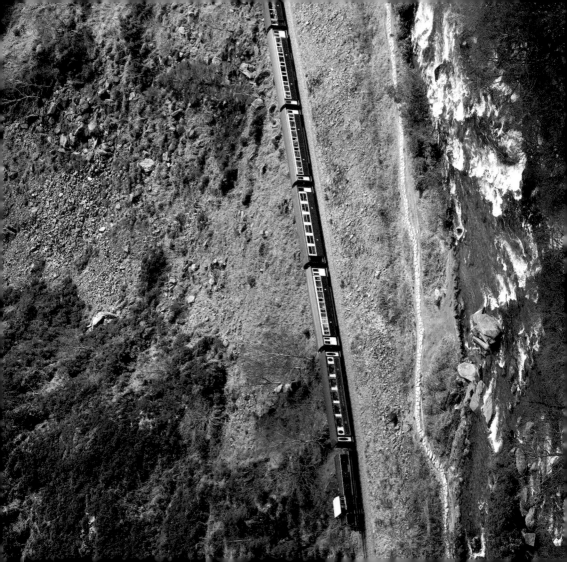

history and a visit to the museum situated by the harbour is a must. As with so many of our heritage railways there's a lot more on offer than just a journey, from Halloween and Santa Trains to Easter frolics there's even an annual Rail Ale festival. A few years ago I had the honour of being invited to open the Rail Ale festival, the mix of music, steam trains and real ale was most enjoyable ... from what I can remember!

To a railway enthusiast one of the main attractions of the Welsh Highland Railway has to be the locomotives. The railway uses massive *Beyer Garratts* which are the largest 2 foot gauge steam locomotives in the world. In fact they are so impressive that we could be forgiven for thinking at first glance that they were standard gauge locomotives.

As I have said earlier the scenery along the journey is truly spectacular, but to me the high point has to be the section that runs alongside the river Glaslyn through the Aberglaslyn pass and tunnels, this alone has to be worth the price of a ticket.

11. Rhyl Miniature Railway

For many of us in northern Wales, growing up in the 1950s and 60s, one of the highlights of the year was the Sunday school trip to Rhyl. Having arrived at our destination there was only one place to go, Marine Lake Amusement Park! Even though the park boasted a rollercoaster, big dipper, ghost train and countless other attractions, there was only one ride that I was truly interested in, and that was the famous Miniature Railway.

Steam hauled, it was always a frantic race to try and sit immediately behind the driver and pretend we were driving.

Built in 1911 the railway is in fact the oldest miniature railway in Britain. Originally designed by Henry Greenly, who thought that the Marine Lake was an ideal place for a miniature line – and how right he was. When the railway was built the only other attractions were boating rides and the water chute. As the lake grew in popularity a thriving fairground was built. Sadly, as a sign of the times, Marine Lake Amusement Park has long since disappeared, but it is still possible to take a nostalgic journey around the lake behind one of the Rhyl-built locomotives.

After the train ride, visitors are encouraged to visit the museum at Central Station and learn more about the story of the railway. There is also an audio visual presentation which I had the privilege and honour of narrating some years ago – I hope you enjoy it!

Even though it's a miniature railway, the website is most definitely up there with the big boys! Full of fascinating facts, information and news. Once again, to all the hardworking and dedicated volunteers who keep the railway running and allow so many of us to relive our youth and hopefully pass the experience onto the next generation, I can only say – Thank you!

12. The Great Orme Tramway

The Great Orme Tramway is the only cable-hauled public road tramway in Britain and has been delighting visitors since it was officially opened in 1902.

The one mile journey begins at Victoria Station and climbs to the halfway station where there is an exhibition covering the history of the tramway and a chance to see the Victorian engineering. Here you will have the opportunity of jumping onto one of the beautifully restored tramcars to complete the journey to the summit. On a clear day it's possible to see as far as the Isle of Man, Blackpool and even the Lake District. There is plenty to do on arrival at the summit including a visit to the Great Orme Visitors Centre, Adventure Playground, Olde Victorian Picture House, Adventure Golf and Randolph Turpin's Bar.

The Great Orme (*Penygogarth*) is also home to several large herds of Kashmiri goats, originally descended from several given by Queen Victoria to Lord Mostyn.

The return journey provides breathtaking views of the town of Llandudno, now the largest seaside resort in northern Wales. It also provides further evidence, if any were needed, as to why the Victorians called it 'Queen of the Welsh resorts'.

13. Conwy Valley Railway Museum and Miniature Railway

There can be no more picturesque and idyllic village in Wales than Betws-y-coed, a view I'm sure that would be supported by the thousands of tourists who visit annually from all over the world. One of the attractions that has become extremely popular is the local railway museum and miniature railway. The centre is situated adjacent to the British Rail station, and even though this book concentrates on our heritage railways I can thoroughly recommend the train service between Llandudno Junction and Betws-y-coed. The journey offers wonderful panoramic views of the Conwy valley as the track at times runs alongside the meandering river Conwy.

Inside the museum there is plenty of

L & N W R Cᵒ
24 A

& N. W. Rʸ

1 IN 74

1 IN 31

LEVEL

LNER MAINTENANCE ENDS

GREAT CENTRAL Rʸ
TRESPASSERS ON THIS PROPERTY WILL BE PROSECUTED.

¼

¼

3

'hands-on' activity with the opportunity of operating a model railway with the push of a button. There are lots of railway artefacts and miniature railway engines, including a magnificent quarter scale model of *Britannia*, one of the last classes of British steam locomotives to be built between 1951 and 1954. In fact the museum offers a comprehensive history of both standard and narrow gauge railways in northern wales.

Outside the museum there's a 7 1/4 inch miniature railway that takes you on a trip around the beautifully landscaped grounds. One cannot fail to be impressed with the amount of hard work undertaken by the owners in extending the line and upgrading the track and rolling stock.

There is also a 15 inch gauge tramcar which runs over a mile section of track parallel with the main Llandudno Junction to Blaenau Ffestiniog line. This gives the museum a unique claim to fame in that it has the only station footbridge in the United Kingdom to span three different gauges of 7 1/4 inch, 15 inch and standard gauge!

Before leaving, a browse in the museum shop is a must as it's full to the brim of model trains, accessories, bocks and souvenirs. Finally what better way to relax at the end of your visit than with tea and cakes in a real buffet car.

14. Vale of Rheidol Railway

The Vale of Rheidol Light Railway was authorised by act of Parliament in 1897. This was to incorporate a line from Aberystwyth to Devil's Bridge as well as a harbour branch. However due to difficulty with raising capital the line did not officially open to passengers until some five years later.

Initially it was thought that the railway would lead to a resurgence in the lead mining industry and some mines were reopened. The ore was then taken to Aberystwyth where it was transported onwards by ship.

In 1912 control of the line passed to the Cambrian Railways. The outbreak of the First World War in 1914 saw the closure of the Rheidol United Lead Mine and passenger services were reduced. The decline in lead mining sadly continued in the years following the war, but this was balanced with an increase in tourist traffic. In 1922 Cambrian Railway was taken over by the Great Western Railway which lead to the closure of the harbour branch and termination of all goods services. Passenger services continued with the line becoming a major tourist attraction, this continued until the outbreak of the Second World War when the line closed completely for the duration of the war. In 1948 ownership of the Vale of Rheidol passed to British Railways and despite threats of closure it became the last steam railway owned by British Rail until it was privatised in 1989. Since then there has been substantial investment in the railway with the restoration of the coal fired locomotives, carriages have also been renovated and more recently the opening up of breathtaking views of the Rheidol

DEVIL'S BRIDGE
(PONTARFYNACH)

valley, which for so many years had been obscured.

The Vale of Rheidol Railway was my first encounter with a narrow gauge railway as an enthusiastic five year old back in 1953. It's not surprising therefore that if I was asked to chose my favourite narrow gauge railway then the Vale of Rheidol would probably be it. Back then the Aberystwyth

terminus of the Vale of Rheidol was adjacent to the main line station along side Park Avenue with its large and handy car park. My junior school, Ysgol Gymraeg Aberystwyth, was literally a stone's throw away and I can vividly remember the shrill whistle of the locomotives piercing through the open classroom window as they started the long haul to Devil's Bridge.

The journey itself takes an hour to cover the 11¾ miles (19 km). The track twists and turns climbing steadily some 700 feet (200 meters) to reach its destination. A few years ago I had the privilege of riding on the footplate of one of the locos and I can assure you that looking out of the cabside on the left hand side and seeing the sheer drop is something that I will never forget. Something else I will never forget is the childhood memory of going fishing on the river Rheidol and seeing the '*trên bach*' approaching in the distance. This would be the sign for us all to down fishing rods and wave to the train as it passed by – it would always respond by giving us a friendly greeting on the whistle!

As a keen railway enthusiast (train spotter!) there was always something magical about the Vale of Rheidol locomotives, as the railway was part of the British Railways network, they were the only narrow gauge locomotives featured in my Ian Allen locospotters book. There were only three locos – *Owain Glyndŵr*, *Llywelyn* and *Prince of Wales*, and it was the

only class of loco that I could boast I had seen the entire class!

Along the journey the train travels through some truly spectacular scenery with the opportunity of stopping along the way at one of the many halts, such as Aberffrwd or Rheidol Falls, and then catching a later train to continue the journey.

On arrival at Devil's Bridge there is the opportunity to visit the famous waterfalls or exploring further the stunning Ceredigion landscape.

As I said the Vale of Rheidol Railway is very close to my heart and I have been particularly impressed with the ways in which the railway has developed and progressed over the years. Carriages now have heating for the winter months and there are special events arranged throughout the year. The railway is to be congratulated, and what makes it even more special to me is the fact that it has not lost any of that magic that I experienced when I first travelled on it all those year ago.

15. The Welshpool and Llanfair Light Railway

Unlike most of the other great little trains of Wales, the Welshpool and Llanfair Light Railway was not built to carry any mineral traffic. Its purpose was to link the local farming communities with the market town of Welshpool which was on the Cambrian Railways main line. The original builders of the Welshpool and Llanfair Railway chose a gauge of 2 foot 6 inches to cope with the tight curves and steep gradient on its journey to Llanfair Caereinion.

Sadly the railway was not to achieve the success that had been hoped. In 1922 both the Cambrian and Welshpool and Llanfair were taken over by the Great Western Railway. One of the strangest things to happen was that in 1925 the Great Western Railway introduced a bus service in competition to the buses that already ran on the route. This lead to even more rail passengers deciding to take the bus. Even so, the railway continued to run a limited and somewhat unremarkable passenger service until 1931 when it finally succumbed to the more regular bus service. Despite the end of passenger services, freight continued to be carried on the line. With the exception of Sundays, one train would run each way carrying mostly coal and a few parcels in the van. However on Mondays there would often be a second train taking livestock to Welshpool market.

Following the nationalisation of the railways in 1948 the line continued to be operated by British Railways until its complete closure in 1956. The same year the Welshpool and Llanfair Railway Preservation Society was established. During the following years a great deal of hard work was undertaken by volunteers and a light railway order was finally granted in 1962. The following year on 6 April, some 30 years after the last public passenger service, the Welshpool and Llanfair Railway was officially reopened. The first trains only ran on the section between Llanfair Caereinion and Castle Caereinion with the extension to Welshpool (Raven Square) being completed in 1981.

The Welshpool and Llanfair Railway has always reminded me of that wonderful 1953 Ealing comedy film *The Titfield Thunderbolt*. The story revolves around a group of locals in an idyllic English village who when faced with plans to close the local branch line decide to run the line themselves. Not wishing to give too much away but the film does have a happy ending, and so it's been with the Welshpool and Llanfair Railway. There is one wonderful scene in the film where an old locomotive is 'borrowed' late at night from the local museum and driven through the streets to the village station. Whenever I see this particular scene it always makes me think of what it must have been like in the early days of the Welshpool and Llanfair Railway when the railway actually ran through the town to its destination at the standard gauge Cambrian station. What a wonderful sight it must have been to see these narrow gauge locomotives weaving their way between houses and shops and crossing busy streets. Even though the first few trains to run during the preservation era

also ran through the town, it was only a matter of months before the council completed its purchase of this particular section and it was finally closed with the terminus now at Welshpool (Raven Square). As a matter of fact in the early 1960s, some wagons were actually hauled up from the British Railway yard at Welshpool by horse, in the dead of night, before the Council removed the rails from the town section.

Like so many of our heritage railways the Welshpool and Llanfair Railway takes the visitor through some of Wales' most impressive scenery. Starting at the edge of the town, the eight-mile journey takes us up the notoriously steep Golfa bank and into the delightful Banwy valley, it then meanders through a charming rural patchwork before reaching its destination in Llanfair Caereinion. The Welshpool and Llanfair Railway is a truly international railway with rolling stock from as far afield as Hungary and Austria, and there is no better way to enjoy the wonderfully idyllic Montgomeryshire countryside than from one of these open balcony carriages.

16. Aberystwyth Cliff Railway

At the northern end of Aberystwyth prom, Constitution Hill rises dramatically from the sea providing spectacular views of Cardigan Bay and the town itself.

The most relaxing way to enjoy the view is to travel by train on the longest funicular electric cliff railway in Britain. It was opened in 1896, and is the work of the engineer Croydon Marks. Operating originally on the water balance system, the 778 feet (237 metres) undulating track and tilted carriage are unique.

It was built to carry Victorian holidaymakers 430 feet (131 metres) to the summit where they would enjoy the delights of Luna Park which in its heyday

The Great Trains of Wales

boasted a bandstand, a glittering ballroom and tea room.

Today's visitors can enjoy the 1985 built Camera Obscura. The massive 14 inch lens makes it possible to experience a panoramic view of over 100 miles (160 km) of coastline, and a thousand square miles of land and see. There is also the Consti restaurant which was opened in 2005 and has become extremely popular for its excellent food set amid a breathtaking setting. As someone who was fortunate enough to be brought up in Aberystwyth, I would often walk with friends to the summit of Constitution Hill, but I cannot ever remember taking the railway. Nowadays, whenever I visit the town, there is no more welcome a sight than the cliff railway, and the 4 mph journey to the summit suits me just fine.'

17. Corris Railway

Corris Railway has the claim to fame of being the first narrow gauge railway in mid Wales. Its origins date back to the 1850s. The line was originally built as a horse and gravity worked tramroad to transport slate from the quarries at Corris Uchaf and Aberllefenni to the nearest point of navigation on the river Dovey. From there the slate would be transported to varying destinations. In the late 1860s the slate was carried direct to the main line standard gauge railway at Machynlleth.

In 1878 the line was taken over by a London company, Imperial Tramways Limited, and three steam locomotives and ten passenger carriages were introduced. For the remainder of the century the railway enjoyed great prosperity, popularity and success as a tourist attraction.

Sadly the 20th century brought with it a decline in the slate industry, and as with so many railways, increasing competition from bus services.

From 1930 onwards not only were passenger services withdrawn but by 1948 goods services were also terminated, as the line became one of the first to be closed by the newly nationalised British Railways.

For further information on the history of the line I can thoroughly recommend Gwyn Briwnant Jones' beautifully written and illustrated book, *Tales of the old Corris* and *A return to Corris*, written by members of the Corris Railway Society.

In 1966 a group of Talyllyn Railway Preservation Society members from the East Midlands formed the Corris Railway Society. Evidence of their hard work and dedication was seen in 1970 with the opening of the first stage of the Corris Railway Museum with demonstration track.

In 1981 Maespoeth engine shed and yard was returned to the railway and the society has transformed it into a well-equipped engine shed and workshop.

Finally in 1985, after many years of hard work and negotiating, the society ran the first train between Maespoeth and Corris after a break of 37 years. However, the railway had to wait until 2002 before it could run a feepaying passenger service.

Now firmly established as one of the

THE CORRIS RAILWAY COMPANY
SWYDDFA GOFRESTREDIG

RHEILFFORDD CORRIS
Agorwyd gan CHRIS AWDRY Llywydd y Gymdeithas
7ed MEHEFIN 2003

Amgueddfa Rheilffordd

CORRIS
Railway
Museum

CORRIS

CORRIS

'Great Little Trains of Wales,' Corris Railway is far from complete, with exciting new projects. Developments include extending the line southwards through Maespoeth junction down the Dulas Valley as far as Tan-y-Coed. Once completed this will give passengers a run of over 2¾ miles (4.5 km) in each direction.

As this ambitious project will require an enormous effort it is not surprising that on the railway's website there is an appeal for volunteers. There is an open invitation for those who wish to don old clothes and are not afraid of manual labour with spade or scythe to join this exciting project. The 'appeal' goes on to add ... 'it's cheaper than joining a gym'! May I also add, it's a lot more enjoyable and rewarding as well!

18. Rhiw Valley Light Railway

The Rhiw Valley Light Railway was founded by railway enthusiast Jack Woodroffe in 1970. The railway is situated in the Rhiw Valley on the B4390 between the villages of Berriew and Manafon. It's not open to the public on a daily basis but does run open days and is available for private bookings. The railway is built onto a 15 inch gauge and the ¾ of a mile (1.2 km) trip takes the visitor round Lower House farm alongside the river Rhiw.

For times of operation it's worth checking their excellent and extremely informative website.

19. Centre for Alternative Technology Railway

The Centre is situated near the town of Machynlleth. The 40 acre (16 ha) site with 7 acres (2.8 ha) of interactive displays is the largest tourist attraction in the area.

Amongst the Centre's numerous facilities is the Water-balanced Funicular Railway opened in May 1992. It's one of the steepest cliff railways in the world with a gradient of 35 degrees, and is in itself an excellent introduction to sustainable technology.

There are two carriages linked together with a steel cable so that when a carriage goes down the other is pulled up. As the carriage makes its way up to the centre the visitor can enjoy breathtaking views of the surrounding mountains and valley. The lake at the top not only supplies water for

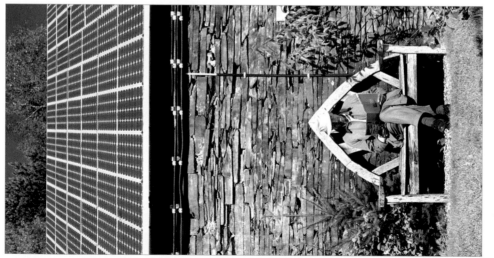

the operation of the railway, but it also provides an attractive feature, stocked with native species of plants and fish.

A day at the Centre is a must if you are visiting the area, as it really does have something for the whole family. Not only can one discover more about the environment and the benefits of renewable energy, but the friendly and helpful staff ensure that it's done in a relaxing and enjoyable way.

20. Brecon Mountain Railway

The Brecon Mountain Railway runs on a section of what used to be the standard gauge line between Brecon and Merthyr. The line was originally opened in 1859 and closed in 1964, but a section of it was chosen in 1972 as a new narrow gauge line. It runs from Pant, which is situated 3 miles (4.8 km) north of Merthyr Tydfil to Torpantau.

As with so many of our heritage railways it was a long and uphill struggle to finally reach the stage in 1980 when the Brecon Mountain Railway (light railway) order was granted.

The reason for the long delay was that the track-bed had been sold to fourteen different landowners, agreement was reached with thirteen but a financial deal could not be agreed with the fourteenth which was the site of Pant station. The new Pant station is actually situated above Morlais tunnel and the smoke vent from the original line can be seen as you enter the new station building.

This is the start of the journey and the station at Pant is one of the most impressive on the Welsh Heritage Railway map. One of the highlights for me is the short walk from the booking hall to the platform which passes a well-equipped maintenance area, where there is opportunity to spend time on a specially constructed gallery overlooking the workshop. From here you can see locomotives and rolling stock being repaired and maintained.

Once on board one of the all-weather observation coaches the journey takes us into the Brecon Beacons National Park along the full length of the Taf Fechan reservoir and uphill passing the nearby Upper Pentwyn reservoir before reaching the summit of the line at Torpantau. All returning trains from Torpantau stop at the intermediate station in Pontsticill where there will be time to visit the lakeside cafe and the newly opened steam museum. There is also an opportunity to go for walks alongside the reservoir and catch a later train back to Pant.

On returning to Merthyr one cannot forget the role the town played in the

history of railways and one man in particular, Richard Trevithick.

Trevithick was an engineer and inventor, born in Cornwall in 1771. In 1802 he patented a new type of pressurised steam engine. On 21 February 1804, spurred on by a bet between Samuel Homfray and Richard Crawshay, Trevithick revealed his locomotive. The locomotive was put on the rails of the Penydarren Tramroad in Merthyr Tydfil. This connected various ironworks to the Glamorganshire Canal at Abercynon. It became the first Steam Locomotive in the world to run on rails hauling a load. Today there is an opportunity to walk the nine

mile Trevithick trail. Along the way markers point out the historical significance of various locations, but there is far more to the trail than a walk through the past. The walk (and here I have to confess that I have only walked part of it) runs down the Taff vale along the river Taff and passes through a variety of habitats – these include an abundance of trees, shrubs and wild flowers as well as birds, insects and small mammals.

As you walk along the trail it is sometimes hard to imagine that this is where it all started. It's quite a claim to fame to be the home of the world's first locomotive hauled railway journey!

21. Barry Tourist Railway

The Barry Tourist Railway is based at Barry Island railway station and platforms. Since December 2009 the railway has been operated by Cambrian Transport and runs trains on approximately thirty days a year with many special events. One of the biggest events has been the 'Barry at War' weekend, which attracts thousands to the town. Also proving extremely popular are the Santa Special trains during the Christmas period; it's recommended to check with the railway's excellent website for running times.

An unusual aspect of the railway is the fact that for several hundred yards across the causeway the line runs alongside the Network Rail track before diverging into separate platforms at Barry Island.

An interesting fact for steam engine enthusiasts is that the line runs near the former Woodham Brothers scrap yard. Back in its heyday Barry Scrap Yard was a

mecca for all rail enthusiasts and became known as the graveyard of steam with 297 withdrawn British Railways steam locomotives being taken there.

What is incredible is that 213 of the locomotives were rescued for the emerging railway preservation movement with over 100 being restored.

Back in the early 90s I had the privilege of spending a day in the company of Dai Woodham as part of a documentary for HTV, reminiscing about his life in the scrap business. In the programme he came over as a genuine unassuming character who was quite taken aback by all the fuss about him as far as the preservation movement was concerned. What also emerged was the fact that Dai was an

extremely successful and shrewd business man; something he was rightly very proud of.

In the past Barry Island has been associated with the Pleasure Park, Butlin's, the wonderful beaches, and most recently the highly successful comedy series 'Gavin & Stacey'. The Barry Tourist Railway should also be added to the list. It has ambitious plans for the future and a visit will certainly give you the opportunity to experience a real life railway in operation and learn about the history of railways in Barry.

You will also have the opportunity of spending a memorable day enjoying the delights of what the locals now fondly call 'Barrybados'!

22. The Gwili Railway

The Gwili Railway runs from Bronwydd, which is situated on the outskirts of Carmarthen, along a short section of the former Carmarthen to Aberystwyth line.

In the early days of the railway, the line served the local farming and wool industries, but sadly following the First World War this traffic declined. The Second World War brought a new lease of life to the railway as it was used to carry ammunition between southern and northern Wales.

In the years following the war, the branch line to Aberaeron and Newcastle Emlyn was closed.

As a young boy 'trainspotting' on Aberystwyth station in the 1950s, I often stood waiting for the arrival of the train from Carmarthen. For some reason it seemed to me that Carmarthen must be a very long way away because I knew the journey took close to three hours. It was much later that I learnt that the distance was in fact only 56 miles (90 km), and that by car it could be covered in half the time. The line was a typical rural branch line in an era when passengers most definitely came first, even if it meant waiting a few minutes for a regular train.

The line did enjoy a brief resurgence during this period with an increase in summer passenger numbers due to the through specials, carrying holidaymakers to the Butlin's holiday camp in Pwllheli. As with so many railway lines during this period, declining numbers meant that the Beeching axe was inevitable, so it was with the Carmarthen to Aberystwyth line, with the last passenger train running on 22 February 1965. However a section did remain open for freight until the early 70s.

The Gwili Railway was officially formed in 1975, and by 1978 the railway had managed to purchase 8 miles (13 km) of track between Abergwili junction and Llanpumsaint. Also at this time, thanks to the dedication and commitment of its volunteers, a short section of the line was reopened from its base at Bronwydd Arms.

A journey on the Gwili Railway takes the visitor back in time to the 1950s and the opportunity to travel in one of the carefully restored corridor coaches. It never ceases to amaze me just how comfortable and luxurious the seating was – even in second class.

Even before the start of your journey,

I would recommend a visit to the beautifully restored signal box which was saved from Llandybie station on the Heart of Wales Line. The signal man will make you feel most welcomed and take great pride in showing you around and explaining how it all works.

Leaving Bronwydd the line climbs steadily along the valley, never far from the river Gwili (I always like to sit on the right hand side!). On arrival at Llwyfan Cerrig there is an opportunity to take the path down to a picnic area situated on the bank of the river, there are also facilities to buy refreshments. For the more energetic, you can walk along a specially created Nature Trail which winds through an old quarry to emerge above the stock sheds.

From Llwyfan Cerrig the line climbs another ¾ of a mile (1.2 km) before reaching the present terminus at Danycoed Halt.

Some 10 years ago I had the privilege of being invited to be President of the Gwili Railway. It's an honour that I am immensely proud of and therefore know from first hand experience just how much work goes into not only the day-to-day running of the railway but also the

planning for the future. At the time of writing the track has been extended all the way down to Abergwili junction, bringing the line up to a total of 4½ miles (7.24 km) in length. It is planned that this section of the railway will be open by 2017.

As well as running a successful heritage railway the Gwili is also very proud of its association with a wide variety of community groups. It believes in engaging with a broad population and whenever is possible support local charities. The railway is very much part of the community and an example of both working together is the annual Bronwydd village summer fete. Some years ago I was invited to open the fete but unfortunately on the plant stall I miss-identified a tomato plant for a geranium. Gasps of disbelief followed with a comment of 'what do you expect from these city types'. Needless to say I have not been invited back!

23. Pontypool and Blaenavon Railway

The line has the destinction of being the highest preserved standard gauge line in the UK. It runs for 2 miles (3 km) from a halt platform opposite the Whistle Inn public house, southwards towards the town of Blaenavon.

The line from Brynmawr to Blaenavon was officially opened in 1866 with the purpose of carrying coal to the Midlands; however a passenger service was added a few years later. From the turn of the century the line served a number of pits and collieries in the area.

By 1874 an extension to Abersychan and Talywain was opened allowing access to the Great Western Railway which went to Newport. By 1941 passenger services had ceased, although, freight continued to be carried until 1954. The Blaenavon to Pontypool section remained and was still in use for coal trains from other mines until 1980 when Big Pit finally closed. That year also saw the formation of the Pontypool and Blaenavon Railway, with train service starting in 1983, running from Furnace Sidings up the steep climb to

Whistle Inn Halt. In May 2010 the line was extended southwards to the site of the former Blaenavon High Level Station, a distance of approximately a 1¼ mile (2 km). A year later the railway constructed a ½ mile (.80 km) branch line to the Big Pit National Coal Museum. All tickets on the line include travel to the museum, where there is no admission charge.

The museum itself offers a wonderful day out for all ages, with facilities to educate and entertain. The world famous Underground Tour is without doubt a never to be forgotten experience. The visitor gets the opportunity to go 300 feet (91 metres) underground with a real miner and see what life was like for the colliers who worked on the coal face. I for one certainly left the museum with a new respect and utmost admiration for those brave men who the Welsh poet Gwilym R. Tilsely described, in his National Eisteddfod chair winning ode, as 'our valiant heroes'.

One only has to read all the five star reviews of the line to realise that the

The Great Trains of Wales

Pontypool and Blaenavon Railway certainly hits the right note. There's a variety of special events that the railway organises including Halloween, Santa and Murder Mystery specials. The friendly and knowledgeable staff are always on hand to help make the day a special one, and as one reviewer wrote, 'an amazing experience – I thoroughly enjoyed it – even though it rained all day.' High praise indeed!

24. Teifi Valley Railway

The story of the Teifi Valley Railway really is a tale of mixed fortunes. One cannot help believing that if it was not for a small band of dedicated, enthusiastic, committed and extremely hard working volunteers this line might not be in operation today.

It is situated in south-western Wales, north of Carmarthen, occupying part of the track-bed of the old Newcastle Emlyn branch line.

Originally run on broad gauge, the aim of the Carmarthen and Cardigan Railway, as the name implies, was to reach Cardigan. In 1864 it had only reached as far as Llandysul; however, in 1872, the line was converted to standard gauge, and in 1881 was leased by the Great Western Railway. Nothing came of the Cardigan scheme but the line was extended as far as Newcastle Emlyn in 1895.

The passenger service was withdrawn in 1952 and in 1973 freight services were discontinued. All that was left were platforms, bridges and a tunnel. It was during this time that attempts were made to preserve a section of the railway as a standard gauge service, but it was not until 1981 that any realistic preservation scheme got underway.

It was decided to run it as a narrow gauge railway, originally from Henllan to Pontprenshitw and eventually as far as Pont Goch. In July 2009, the Henllan platform was relocated to the original Great Western Railway location. Sadly this was also the year that matters took a turn for the worse for the railway. This period of the line's history is well documented on their excellent website. However, towards the end of 2014 a new chapter began for the Teifi Valley Railway when a new group took over the management of the railway and as of May 2016 track re-laying had reached as far as Forest Halt and train operations had resumed.

Most preserved railways will tell you that during their history they have had many a setback, it seems to be par for the course, but I'm sure that not many would disagree that the Teifi Valley Railway has had more than its fair share.

It may not share in the success of some of the other railways featured in this book,

but against all odds it has survived. It may well be a work in progress, but with an increase in membership and new volunteers things are certainly looking brighter and more promising than they have done for some time. By visiting the railway you are supporting it, and you will also be guaranteed the warmest of welcomes.

COMPACT CYMRU

COMPACT CYMRU
– MORE TITLES;
128 PAGES
£5.95
FULL OF COLOUR IMAGES
AND CONCISE WRITING

Battles FOR Wales

Maddin ap Dafydd

Welsh Pub Names

Welsh Place Names EXPLAINED

Llŷn
the peninsula and its past EXPLORED

Pembrokeshire
its present and its past EXPLORED

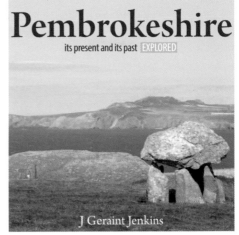

J Geraint Jenkins

Smugglers in Wales EXPLORED

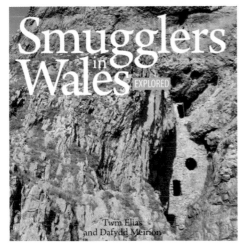

Twm Elias
and Dafydd Meirion

Strait Stories
Menai Strait EXPLORED from Caernarfon to Beaumaris

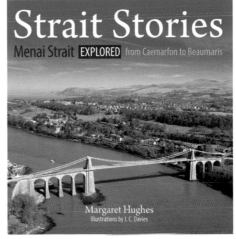

Margaret Hughes
Illustrations by J. C. Davies